Let's Get Crafty with Cardboard & Paint

Let's Get **Crafty** with **Cardboard & Paint**

CICO**kidz**

Published in 2016 by CICO Books
An imprint of Ryland Peters & Small Ltd
20–21 Jockey's Fields   341 E 116th St
London WC1R 4BW   New York, NY 10029

www.rylandpeters.com

10 9 8 7 6 5 4 3 2 1

A CIP catalog record for this book is available from
the Library of Congress and the British Library.

ISBN: 978 1 78249 383 9

Printed in China

Editor: Katie Hardwicke
Designer: Eoghan O'Brien
Photographer: Terry Benson
Stylist: Emily Breen

In-house editor: Dawn Bates
In-house designer: Fahema Khanam
Art director: Sally Powell
Head of production: Patricia Harrington
Publishing manager: Penny Craig
Publisher: Cindy Richards

For additional photography credits, see page 80.

Contents

Introduction

CARDBOARD IS THE PERFECT STARTING POINT FOR GETTING CRAFTY WITH YOUNG CHILDREN. WITH SIMPLE, INEXPENSIVE MATERIALS—MANY OF WHICH CAN BE FOUND IN THE RECYCLING BOX—A LITTLE IMAGINATION, AND SOME CUTTING OUT HELP, THEY'LL BE CREATING TOYS, GIFTS, DECORATIONS, AND ARTWORKS THAT WILL GIVE THEM A HUGE SENSE OF ACHIEVEMENT, WITH LOTS OF FUN ALONG THE WAY.

Getting crafty is the ideal activity for rainy afternoons, mid-morning lulls, play dates, and party planning, and in this book you'll find plenty of ideas and inspiration for fun craft activities that you can enjoy together.

Cardboard lends itself to construction and the Toy Town project on page 68, Cardboard Castle on page 44, or the Doll House Furniture on page 30, are perfect starting points for budding designers. There are endless uses for cardboard tubes: for playtime fun try the Toy Plane on page 26, the Collapsible Telescope on page 70, the Kaleidoscope on page 46, or blast off with the Space Rocket on page 38. You'll find lots of ideas for practical makes, too—try the Tissue Box Desk Organizer on page 22, Bird Feeder on page 36, or the Greetings Card Box on page 58. Making party or festive decorations is a great way to keep over-excited little ones occupied; try the Flower Rolls on page 63, or the Spooky Rolls on page 54 for a Halloween theme. The Shoebox Theater on page 51 will inspire storytelling for those who enjoy a little drama, and you can make Lenny Lion puppet (page 48) or the articulated Daisy Doll (page 41) to star in the show.

Using scissors, pens, glue, paintbrushes, and simple construction are all great ways for young children to develop fine motor skills and coordination. While many projects will only need light adult supervision, there are some steps that will require your help. We have marked these with a helping hands symbol as a guide. Working as a team is all part of the fun and your child will enjoy spending time with you and learning from you, as you get crafty together.

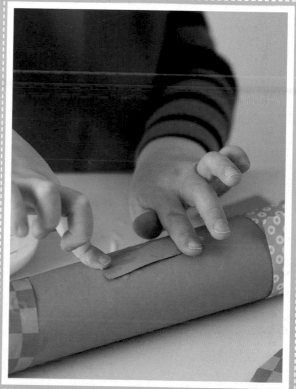

WHAT YOU WILL NEED

For all the projects you will need some basic craft materials. Keep a dedicated corner or drawer for storing your equipment, and stock up on a few craft items for the finishing touches—a good supply of googly eyes is essential! Using cardboard as the starting point for these projects means that you can often find what you need in the recycling box—paper towel tubes, cereal boxes, packaging, greetings cards, and the like can all be transformed into fun creations.

BASIC EQUIPMENT

- Pencils, ruler, and eraser
- White and colored construction paper
- Card for templates
- Tracing paper
- Craft scissors
- Sharp paper scissors and craft knife
- Acrylic paints and paintbrushes
- Felt-tipped pens or marker pens
- Coloring pencils
- White/PVA glue and spreader or brush
- Glue stick
- Masking tape
- Sticky tape
- Paper plates
- Paper towels

RECYCLING BOX

- Large cardboard rolls (paper towels)
- Small cardboard rolls (toilet paper)
- Potato chip or cookie tubes
- Cereal boxes and food packaging
- Cardboard boxes and corrugated cardboard
- Egg cartons
- Gift wrap and greetings cards
- Newspapers and magazines
- Plastic containers
- Fabric scraps

CRAFT MATERIALS

- Glitter
- Sequins, gems, and beads
- Wooden shapes
- Colored or patterned duct tape
- Stickers
- Feathers
- Pompoms
- Yarn
- Buttons, ribbons, and braid
- Felt and fabric
- Tissue paper
- Pipe cleaners
- Googly eyes
- Cotton balls

GETTING MESSY!

Much of the fun of crafting is the chance to get messy, and to make some mess! Follow these tips before you begin for stress-free crafting:

- Cover your work table with newspaper or a wipe-down sheet or tablecloth
- Protect your child's clothes with an apron or old t-shirt (you may want to do the same!)
- Roll up sleeves and tie long hair out of the way
- Keep a roll of paper towels close by
- When using glitter or sprinkles, put a sheet of paper or newspaper beneath the project and use it to pour the excess glitter back into the pot afterward

CLEARING UP!

Ask your child to help to clear up afterward—washing up paintbrushes and pots will appeal to all those who love to play with water!

- Put all lids back on glue pots, paint pots and tubes, and felt-tipped pens
- Wash paintbrushes and palettes; stand paintbrushes in a jar to dry
- Throw away newspaper and wipe down surfaces
- Throw away little scraps of paper but keep larger pieces for future activities, or put them in the recycling box
- Put any equipment away in drawers or boxes to keep it organized and easy to find next time

TECHNIQUES

CUTTING OUT

Using scissors to cut a straight line is a skill that most young children can master with children's craft scissors. However, several of the projects require you to cut out detailed shapes and we have suggested that an adult help with these stages, either guiding your child or cutting out yourself. Here are a few tips to make cutting out easier and safer:

• Cutting rounded or detailed shapes: hold the scissors steady in one place and let your other hand move the paper as you cut, rather than moving the scissors.

• Cutting windows or holes: to cut out a window or hole from the center of a shape, use the point of the scissors to pierce the paper in the center of the shape, cut a slit to the inner edge, then cut out around the inner edge to remove the shape.

• Cutting circles: some projects require you to cut circles. This is quite tricky for little hands, and even big hands: keep the scissors in one place and turn the paper as you cut, or alternatively draw around a button, bobbin, or other round object first to make a template, then cut out.

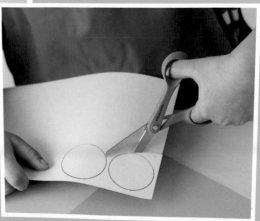

MAKING TEMPLATES

For some projects you need to transfer the template shape given on pages 74–79 onto card, before using it to cut out the final shape from the material used in the project. Use a photocopier to enlarge or reduce the shape if required, following the percentage given with the template.

1 Once the template is the right size, place a sheet of tracing paper over the template outline and hold in place with masking tape. Trace over the lines with a hard pencil.

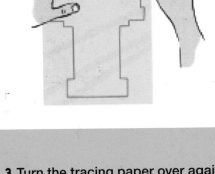

2 Turn the tracing paper over so that the back is facing you and neatly scribble over the lines with a softer pencil. Make sure all the lines are covered.

3 Turn the tracing paper over again so that the top is facing you and position it on your card, using masking tape to hold it in place. Carefully draw over the lines you made in Step 1 with the hard pencil, then remove the tracing paper. The outline will be transferred to the card. Cut out the card template to use for your project.

4 Alternatively, you can photocopy the template directly onto thin card and cut out.

◤ USING TEMPLATES

You may need to help your child when drawing around a template:

- Hold the template in place firmly

- Use a pencil or marker pen to draw around the edge of the template onto the card or paper used in the project

- Keep the pencil upright and draw a steady, continuous line

- Use a white pencil on dark paper or card so that the outline will show clearly

- On felt, a fine-tipped marker or felt-tipped pen may be easier to see

Egg Carton Creature

ALL YOU NEED IS A LITTLE IMAGINATION FOR THIS PROJECT, AND AN EGG CARTON—WE USED A LARGE CARTON BUT A SMALL ONE WOULD WORK JUST AS WELL. GO TO TOWN WITH PAINT AND DECORATIONS TO MAKE YOUR CREATURES AS CUTE OR SCARY AS YOU LIKE.

WHAT YOU WILL NEED

- Templates on page 77
- Large cardboard egg carton
- Acrylic paint
- Paintbrush
- Pencil and colored paper
- Scissors
- Felt-tipped pens or marker pens
- White/PVA glue
- Googly eyes
- Craft pompoms, pipe cleaners

PAINT CARTON Prepare your work surface for painting. Paint the egg carton all over, top and bottom. Let the egg carton dry. You may need two coats for complete coverage.

MAKE EYES While the egg carton is drying, make the eyes. Copy the templates on page 77 and cut out circles from colored paper—we made two sets of eyes on green and yellow paper.

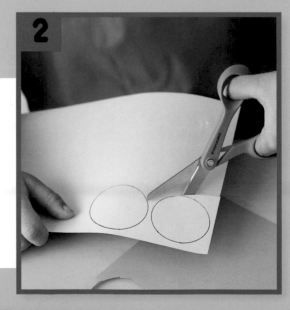

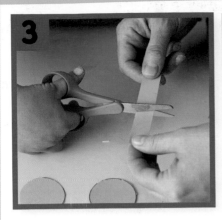

MAKE TEETH
Use the template on page 77 to cut out some pointed teeth at the end of two strips of colored paper. Put a small dab of glue on the back of one colored paper eye and stick it to the carton.

ADD THE FACE Stick a different-colored eye on the top, slightly off-center. Repeat for the other eyes.

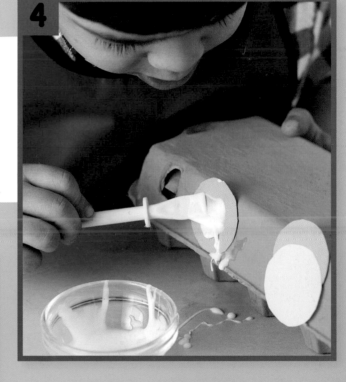

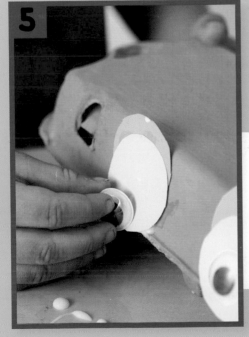

FINISH EYES Glue googly eyes on top of the paper circles and position the pupils in different places to give your creature a fun expression.

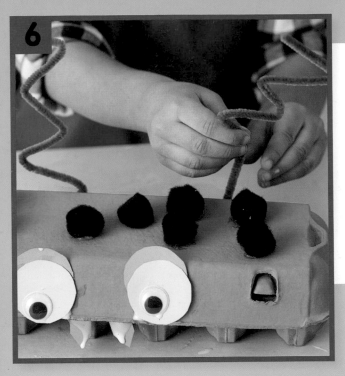

6

DECORATE Glue the teeth to the inside of the lid, between the eyes. You can make your egg carton creature even scarier by decorating his body—try painting or drawing on scales, adding antennae, arms, or legs with pipe cleaners, or covering the carton with pompoms or yarn to make a furry monster.

Apple Tree

ENHANCE PLAYTIME OR STORYTIME WITH IMAGINATIVE PROPS LIKE THIS SWEET APPLE TREE—PERFECT FOR A FAIRY GATHERING OR TO ADD SOME GREEN SPACES TO THE TOY TOWN PROJECT ON PAGE 68. YOU COULD ADAPT THIS IDEA TO MAKE A TREE FOR EACH SEASON, USING PAINT, STICKERS, OR EVEN REAL LEAVES TO DECORATE IT.

WHAT YOU WILL NEED

- Templates on page 74
- Cardboard box
- Scissors
- Acrylic paint
- Paintbrush
- Craft knife
- Stickers and craft pompoms or other craft items, like buttons and beads, for the apples
- White/PVA glue
- Green card
- 3 small cardboard tubes
- Paper clips

1

TRACE SHAPES Copy the tree shape on page 74, cut out, and draw around the template twice on the side of the box. Alternatively, draw the shapes freehand. Cut out the shapes.

PAINT TREE Use bright green to paint the tree shapes on both sides, covering the edges too, if the cardboard is thick. Let the paint dry and add another coat if you need to.

2

SLOT TOGETHER Cut a long slit down the center of one tree shape, stopping about 2in (5cm) from the top, and slot it over the other shape to join them together.

DECORATE TREE Have fun raiding your craft supplies to decorate the tree with "apples"—use glue to stick on beads, pompoms, buttons, or stickers.

MAKE LEAVES Copy the leaf template on page 74, cut it out, and draw around it on the green card several times. Cut out the leaves and glue these onto each side of the tree top.

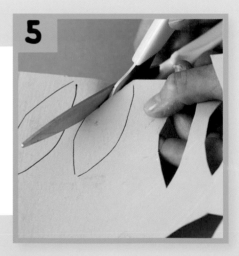

MAKE TREE TRUNK Paint the cardboard tubes in brown and let dry. Glue the tubes together, using paper clips to hold them in place while they dry. Remove the paper clips.

7

ASSEMBLE TREE Snip triangles from the top of the cardboard roll trunk, then slot the tree into the spaces to join the trunk and tree top.

Crafty Tip

Use pretty flower buttons or scrunched-up balls of pastel-colored tissue paper to decorate your tree with spring blossom.

Magnetic Bookmark

THIS HANDY DECORATIVE BOOKMARK IS CUT FROM THE FOLDED EDGES OF A CEREAL PACKET AND IS FINISHED WITH PRETTY PATTERNED PAPER, THEN TRIMMED WITH DECORATIVE EDGE SCISSORS. THE BOOKMARKS WOULD MAKE LOVELY GIFTS OR PARTY FAVORS.

WHAT YOU WILL NEED

- Cereal box
- Scissors
- Patterned paper or gift wrap
- White/PVA glue
- Pinking shears or decorative craft scissors
- Self-adhesive magnetic strip

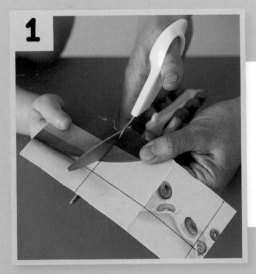

CUT OUT CARD Cut out a rectangular shape from the cereal box, cutting cross the folded edge, so that you have a piece of card measuring approximately 4 x 2in (10 x 5cm), with a fold running through the middle. This is your bookmark.

CUT OUT PATTERNED PAPER Cut out a piece of patterned paper the same size as the bookmark— trace around the bookmark to match the size.

3

GLUE TOGETHER Place the bookmark flat on your work surface and glue the patterned paper to the front. Press the paper flat to make sure the edges are bonded, then let the glue dry completely.

4

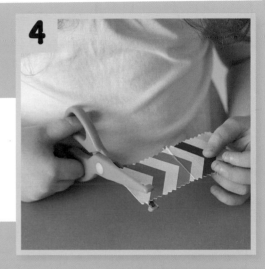

CUT DECORATIVE EDGE Cut all the way around the edges of the bookmark using pinking shears or decorative craft scissors.

ADD MAGNET
Cut a piece of magnetic strip. Peel the backing paper off the strip and stick one on the inside of the bookmark, near the bottom. Stick a second piece to the opposite side.

5

The magnets hold the bookmark in place with the pages in between.

Tissue Box Desk Organizer

WHAT YOU WILL NEED

- Empty tissue box
- Duct tape (look for colored or patterned tape and use an assortment)
- Scissors
- 2 small cardboard tubes
- 1 large cardboard tube

THIS ACTIVITY IS GREAT FUN, WITH LOTS OF STICKY TAPE AND STICKERS—AND NO MESS! HELP YOUR CHILD TO MEASURE OUT THE LENGTHS OF TAPE AND THEN THEY CAN STICK THE PIECES IN PLACE INDEPENDENTLY. TO FINISH, THEY CAN RAID THEIR STICKER STASH FOR DECORATING THEIR DESK TIDY JUST HOW THEY LIKE IT.

COVER TOP Hold one end of the duct tape on one side of the tissue box and pull it across the top to measure the length needed. Trim the tape and stick in place—older children can cut the tape, while younger ones can help to measure the length. Cover the top but make sure you keep the open hole at the top clear of tape.

COVER SIDES Next, attach the end of the duct tape to the top side of the box and pull the duct tape along and cut a strip, gently pressing on it to stick it down. Cover all four sides in this way. You don't need to cover the bottom as it won't be seen, but you can if you want to! Use different patterned tape if you have some.

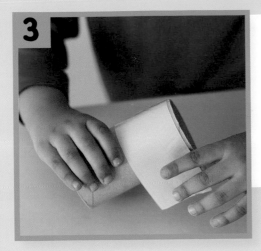

3

COVER TUBES For the pen holders, take a small tube and stick a strip of duct tape around the top of the tube. Add another strip of duct tape all around the tube, this time sticking it just under the first strip of tape. Add more duct tape so that you are creating a striped effect. Repeat to cover the other cardboard tubes.

4

ADD TUBES Insert the covered tubes one by one into the top opening of the tissue box. They will stand up on their own.

5

ADD STICKERS Choose your favorite stickers to decorate the box, or add ribbons, coloring, cut-out pictures, or photographs to personalize your box. Now you're ready to fill the tubes with all your craft supplies and desk accessories.

Rainstick

WITH A FEW SIMPLE MATERIALS, YOU CAN CREATE AN AUTHENTIC VERSION OF THE TRADITIONAL PERUVIAN RAINSTICK. WITH DRIED RICE OR BEANS THE SHAKER BECOMES A FUN MUSICAL INSTRUMENT OR SIMPLY ADDS A NOISY ELEMENT TO PLAYTIME!

WHAT YOU WILL NEED

- Sturdy cardboard tube (a postal tube or potato chip package work well)
- Brown wrapping paper (optional)
- Sticky tape
- White/PVA glue
- Aluminum foil
- Small cup of dried beans or uncooked rice
- Sheets of colored paper
- Sticky-backed gems or felt-tipped pens (optional)

SEAL TUBE Postal tubes usually come with a plastic cap. If yours does, glue the cap in place at one end. If it doesn't, use a piece of cardboard and tape instead. If you are using a potato chip tube, use a piece of paper to cover the tube, wrapping it around and gluing along one edge to secure.

MAKE COIL Take a long piece of aluminum foil that's about twice the length of your cardboard tube. Scrunch and roll it up tightly to make a long snake shape, then wrap it around your arm to make a coil. Push the coil into your tube.

ADD BEANS Pour the uncooked beans or rice into the open end of the tube, then seal the end of your rainstick as you did in Step 1.

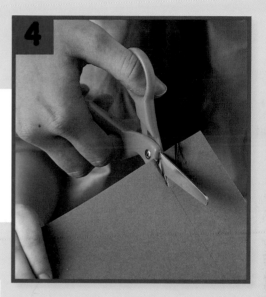

CUT STRIPS Draw and cut out strips of paper to decorate the tube. We used colored paper strips to make a rainbow effect, but you could cover the tube in a single sheet of paper, or add stickers, paint, or pens to decorate.

DECORATE Glue the strips in place, or attach with sticky tape. To add more embellishment, decorate with gems or stickers, and draw or paint a design.

Crafty Tip

To play your rainstick, simply tip it to a 45-degree angle. As you tip the rainstick, turn it slightly to keep the sound going for a longer time. You can also use it as a shaker.

Toy Plane

CARDBOARD TUBES ARE THE PERFECT STARTING POINT FOR ALL KINDS OF VEHICLES, ESPECIALLY PLANES AND ROCKETS! HERE, WITH JUST A COUPLE OF STRIPS OF CARDBOARD AND SOME CRAFT STICKS, YOUR CHILD CAN DESIGN THEIR OWN BI-PLANE WITH HAND-PAINTED LIVERY.

WHAT YOU WILL NEED

- Large cardboard tube
- Cardboard
- Card pot (yogurt carton or fiber plant pot)
- Acrylic paint
- Paintbrush
- Scissors
- White/PVA glue
- Craft sticks
- Sheets of colored paper
- Stickers or buttons to decorate

1

GATHER MATERIALS Find all the different pieces of card to make your plane—look in the recycling box for a cardboard tube, a box, and a pot made from card, such as a yogurt carton or a fiber plant pot.

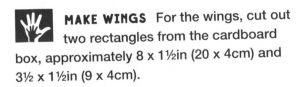 **MAKE WINGS** For the wings, cut out two rectangles from the cardboard box, approximately 8 x 1½in (20 x 4cm) and 3½ x 1½in (9 x 4cm).

2

3

PAINT WINGS AND BODY Choose your plane's livery colors and paint the cardboard tube and the wings. Make sure that you paint both sides of the wings. Let the paint dry.

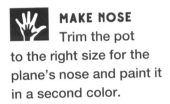

MAKE NOSE Trim the pot to the right size for the plane's nose and paint it in a second color.

4

5

ASSEMBLE PLANE Glue the nose cone to the top of the cardboard tube. Glue the long wings in the middle of the tube, making sure that the wings are centered. Attach the smaller wings at the end of the tube.

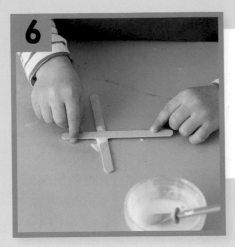

MAKE PROPELLERS Put a dab of glue in the center of one craft stick and attach the other stick to make an "X" shape. Let the glue dry.

FINISHING TOUCHES Glue the propellers to the front of the plane's nose—try to position them so that the plane rests on them to lift the nose off the ground.

DECORATE PLANE Now you can add some windows and other embellishments. Glue little squares of colored paper or mirror card on the sides for windows, and put stickers or buttons on the wing tips. You're ready for take off!

Crafty Tip

Make a runway for your plane from the side of a large cardboard box—draw or paint on lines for the runway. You could add airport buildings, too; see the Toy Town project on page 68, for some ideas.

Decoupage Box

WHAT YOU WILL NEED

- Cardboard box
- Assorted decorative papers, gift wrap, or decoupage scraps
- White/PVA glue
- Paintbrush
- Scissors
- Decorative craft scissors
- Glitter (optional)

DECOUPAGE IS A SIMPLE TECHNIQUE OF LAYERING AND GLUING SCRAPS OF PAPER TO MAKE A PICTURE OR PATTERN. HERE, WE'VE COVERED A CARDBOARD BOX WITH A CUPCAKE THEME, USING PAPER LINERS, DOILIES, AND GIFT WRAP TO MAKE A PRETTY BED FOR TEDDY!

GATHER MATERIALS Gather together your box and pieces of paper. We used paper cupcake liners, doilies, tissue paper, and gift wrap.

START GLUING First stick on larger pieces of paper to cover the box completely. Allow the glue to dry before applying the next layer of paper. Then add smaller pieces. Allow some drying time between layers, so the wet glue does not cause the layer beneath to peel away. Keep adding to your design. We cut out cupcake images from gift wrap using decorative scissors to give the pieces a pretty edge.

ADD GLITTER For a bit of sparkle, you could add a dab of glue and sprinkle over some glitter.

Doll House Furniture

USE RECYCLED MATCHBOXES, CARDBOARD, AND CRAFT STICKS TO MAKE THIS DELIGHTFUL COLLECTION OF DOLL HOUSE FURNITURE. YOUR CHILD WILL BE HAPPILY ABSORBED IN DESIGNING THIS BEDROOM SET THAT WILL GIVE THEM HOURS OF PLAYTIME FUN ONCE THE PAINT HAS DRIED.

WHAT YOU WILL NEED

FOR THE DRESSING TABLE
- Templates on page 78
- 8 small empty matchboxes
- White/PVA glue
- 2 different shades of acrylic paint
- Paintbrush
- 8 small beads for knobs
- Piece of card
- Scissors
- Metallic card

FOR THE BED
- Egg carton
- Corrugated cardboard
- 3 craft sticks
- Beads
- Acrylic paint and paintbrush
- Glue

TO MAKE THE DRESSING TABLE

GLUE MATCHBOXES TOGETHER Apply a layer of glue to the bottom of the first matchbox and stick to one of the other matchboxes, pressing down firmly. Add another two matchboxes to make a cabinet with four drawers. Make a matching set of drawers for the other side. Let the glue dry completely.

PAINT MATCHBOXES Remove the inner trays from the matchboxes (the drawers). Paint the outside of the matchbox stack and let dry completely. You may need to apply a second coat of paint for complete coverage.

PAINT DRAWERS Paint the four drawers using the second shade of paint and let dry completely. Again, you may need to apply a second coat of paint for complete coverage. Repeat Steps 2 and 3 to paint the matching drawers for the other side.

ADD BEADS Put a dab of glue on the front of a painted drawer and stick a bead in place as a handle.

Crafty Tip

Gift wrap, origami paper, patterned craft paper, and even scraps of real wallpaper, can be used to line a cardboard box to make a room set for your furniture.

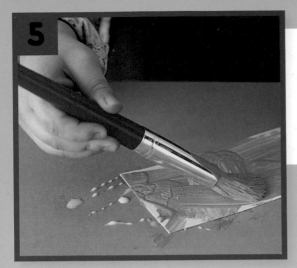

5

6

MAKE TABLE Copy the templates on page 78 for the top of the dressing table and the mirror frame onto card and cut them out. Paint both pieces to match the outside of the drawers.

MAKE MIRROR Copy the template for the mirror and cut out from a piece of metallic or shiny card. Glue the mirror to the center of the mirror frame.

7

ATTACH MIRROR Fold the edge of the mirror in by ½in (1cm) to make a frame, then stick the mirror to the back of the table top with sticky tape. Glue the table top to the drawers.

TO MAKE THE BED

MAKE BED Paint the top of an egg carton box. Using a different color, paint the craft sticks and let everything dry completely.

8

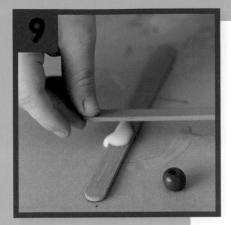

ASSEMBLE BED Glue the craft sticks together to make the headboard, positioning two vertical sticks at the side and joining them with one horizontal stick at the top. Add some beads to decorate. Glue the headboard to the bed base.

MAKE BEDDING Cut a small piece of corrugated cardboard for the pillow. Paint it white and glue to the top of the bed. Cut a piece of corrugated card slightly larger than the bed base and paint in a color to match the bedroom décor. Stick to the bed base.

MAKE EXTRA FURNITURE For the stool, paint a cardboard tube inside and out and cut in half. Cut out a circle from card about 3in (7.5cm) in diameter and paint to match the bedding. Glue together. Make an extra set of drawers for the bedside table. To make the room, cut the top and one side from a cardboard box. Paint the floor and paper the walls with gift wrap.

Travel Desk

THIS LITTLE TRAVEL DESK IS PERFECT FOR CAR JOURNEYS OR VACATIONS—IT'S GREAT FOR KEEPING TOY CARS, SNACKS, GAMES, OR CRAYONS FROM FALLING UNDER YOUR FEET WHILE YOU ARE ON A ROAD TRIP AND PROVIDES A USEFUL SURFACE FOR GAMES OR COLORING ON THE GO.

WHAT YOU WILL NEED

- 1 large, family-sized cereal box
- Craft knife
- Scissors
- Ruler
- Marker pens
- Paper or paints and paintbrush
- Duct tape (optional)
- Stickers (optional)

1

CUT AWAY TOP Put the cereal box flat on your work surface. Using a craft knife, cut around the outside rectangle of the cereal box, leaving a small border, and then remove the rectangle. Use the scissors carefully to neaten the edges. Set aside the cut-away cardboard rectangle in your art area.

PAINT BOX Cover your box with paper or paint, covering the sides and the base. You may need two coats of paint to cover the cereal box design. Let the paint dry.

2

3

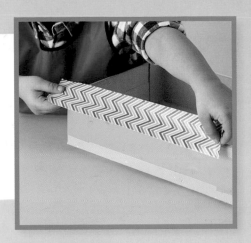

ADD TAPE To strengthen your box, add strips of duct tape along the cut edges and around the sides.

DECORATE If you like, you can decorate your box further with stickers, ribbons, cut-out pictures, or recycled maps.

4

5

DRAW INSIDE Using marker pens, draw on the inside of the travel desk—try road lines or train tracks, a house with rooms, a city with buildings, parks, and roads, or leave it blank and use it as a work surface for coloring.

Crafty Tip

You can re-use the cut-away rectangle to make the Felt Story Board activity on page 72.

Bird Feeder

YOUNG CHILDREN WILL LOVE THIS MESSY ACTIVITY! THIS SIMPLE BIRD FEEDER CAN HANG FROM A TREE IN THE GARDEN AND WILL SOON ATTRACT WILDLIFE AND BIRDS THAT YOU CAN WATCH FROM A WINDOW TOGETHER.

WHAT YOU WILL NEED

- Birdseed (a mixture of seeds such as sunflower or pumpkin work fine too)
- 2 plates
- Peanut butter (or nut-free spread)
- Small cardboard tube
- String or twine
- Scissors

MEASURE OUT SEED Pour a small quantity of the birdseed onto a plate—you'll need about three tablespoons to make one bird feeder.

SPREAD This is the messy bit! Put a tablespoon of peanut butter or nut-free spread onto another plate. Take your cardboard tube and use the back of the spoon to cover it with the peanut butter or nut-free spread. Add more peanut butter if needed to make sure all of the tube is covered.

ROLL IN SEEDS Hold the tube by the ends and place it in the plate of birdseed. Gently roll it back and forth so that the birdseed sticks to the peanut butter. Make sure you cover the entire tube in birdseed.

ADD HANGING LOOP Cut a length of string approximately 12in (30cm) long. Thread the string through the tube and tie a double knot at the ends to secure it. Now you are ready to go outside and hang your bird feeder to a branch.

Crafty Tip

Make sure that your birdseed mix includes some sunflower seeds, so that you will attract as many different birds as possible.

Space Rocket

THIS CREATIVE ACTIVITY WILL KEEP ALL SPACE FANS HAPPILY ABSORBED DESIGNING THEIR VERY OWN ROCKET, USING THE INNER TUBE OF A ROLL OF PAPER TOWELS. WITH STREAMS OF TISSUE-PAPER FLAMES, THIS ACTIVITY INSTANTLY TRANSFORMS INTO AN IMAGINATIVE TOY THAT'S READY FOR TAKE-OFF.

WHAT YOU WILL NEED

- Large cardboard tube
- Sheet of colored paper
- White/PVA glue
- Decorative paper
- Thin card
- Cardboard pot or fiber plant pot
- Paint and paintbrush
- Orange, yellow, and red tissue paper

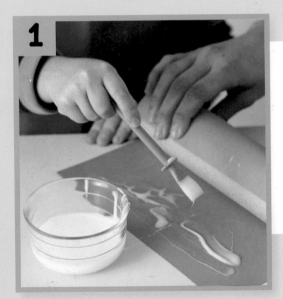

1

COVER TUBE Cut a piece of paper to the height of the cardboard tube, and allowing for an overlap of about 1in (2.5cm) on the longer edge. Roll the paper around the tube and glue in place along the edge. Allow the glue to dry.

CUT SHAPES Cut the decorative paper to make the band at the bottom of the rocket and cut paper for the windows. You can also use craft foam shapes or found objects, like bottle tops.

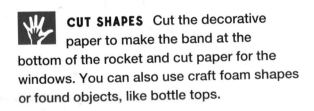

2

3

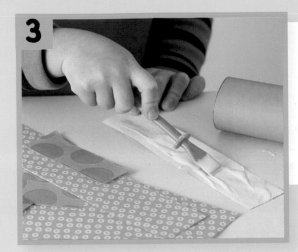

GLUE SHAPES Apply some glue to the back of each shape and stick them to the cardboard tube, pressing each piece flat as you go.

4

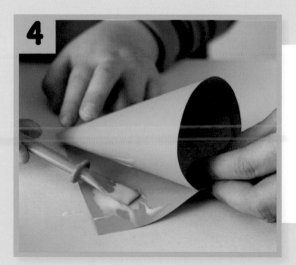

MAKE NOSE CONE From the thin card, cut out a semicircle with a 6in (15cm) diameter. Fold the piece of card into a cone shape and glue in place along the edge. Glue the cone to the top of the tube.

5

MAKE ROCKET BLASTERS Cut out triangles around the top edge of a fiber plant pot to create a fin shape.

6

PAINT BLASTERS Add a generous layer of paint to the inside and outside of the rocket blasters and let them dry. Glue the blasters to the base of the rocket.

7

ADD TISSUE PAPER FLAMES Tear, or cut, lengths of orange, yellow, and red tissue paper measuring about 12in (30cm) long, and glue them to the inside of the base to create the rocket's flames. You're ready for blast off!

Crafty Tip

Use metallic paper and aluminum foil to decorate your rocket and give it a sleek, space-age look.

Daisy Doll

WITH MOVING ARMS, LEGS, AND HEAD, THIS FUN PUPPET CAN DANCE, SING, AND PLAY ALONG WITH YOUR CHILD AND THEIR FRIENDS. USE THE TEMPLATES AS A STARTING POINT FOR LOTS OF DIFFERENT CHARACTERS—YOU COULD USE FABRICS, RIBBONS, AND FELT TO MAKE CLOTHES, TOO.

WHAT YOU WILL NEED

- Templates on page 76
- Pencil and scissors
- Card
- Acrylic paint
- Paintbrush
- Modeling dough
- Metal paper fasteners
- Yarn for hair
- White/PVA glue
- Felt-tipped pens or marker pens
- Buttons

1

CUT OUT Copy the templates on page 76 and cut out the different shapes from stiff cardboard.

PAINT Put different colors of paint in separate dishes and paint each separate shape, washing your brush when changing color. Make sure the paint covers the entire surface—you may need a second coat. Let the paint dry completely.

2

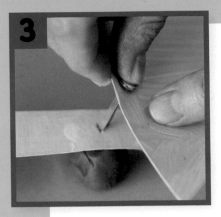

3

ASSEMBLE Attach the hands to the arms and the shoes to the legs by pushing a metal fastener through (see photo opposite for positioning). Put a piece of modeling dough beneath the shape and push the fastener through the card into the dough. Remove the dough and open out the fastener. Do the same to attach the head, arms, and legs to the dress.

4

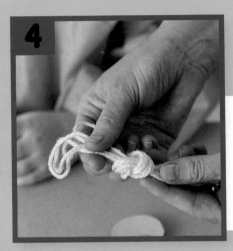

ADD HAIR Cut lengths of yarn and tie in a knot in the middle. Snip the ends. Glue to the head.

5

DRAW FACE Draw on the eyes and mouth with felt-tipped pens or markers. Give your doll a happy smile!

6

DECORATE Glue on some pretty buttons to decorate Daisy's dress and shoes. She's ready to play!

Crafty Tip

Make different outfits by drawing simple shapes, like a T-shirt or shorts, on the card before cutting out and painting.

Cardboard Castle

THIS PROJECT IS SURPRISINGLY EASY TO CONSTRUCT—IT REQUIRES ADULT HELP TO CUT OUT THE PIECES FROM STIFF CARDBOARD, BUT YOUR CHILD WILL LOVE SLOTTING THE PIECES TOGETHER TO BUILD THE CASTLE IN A FEW SIMPLE STEPS. ONCE MADE, THE CASTLE IS A BLANK CANVAS FOR CUSTOMIZING WITH DECORATIONS AND TOYS, AND WILL PROVIDE HOURS OF IMAGINATIVE PLAY.

WHAT YOU WILL NEED

- Templates on page 75
- Pencil
- Scissors
- Scraps of corrugated cardboard
- Craft knife
- Metal ruler
- Cutting mat
- Felt-tipped pens, marker pens, or crayons

1

MAKE TEMPLATES Enlarge the castle templates on page 75 and then cut them all out. Remember to cut out the doors and windows, too.

TRACE TEMPLATES Place each template on the smooth side of a scrap piece of corrugated cardboard, then draw around it using a pencil.

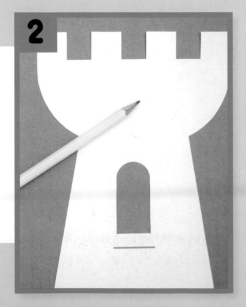

2

3

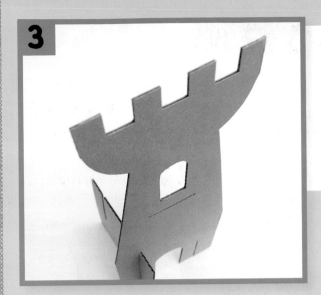

🖐 **CUT OUT SHAPES** Cut out the castle shapes, doors, windows, and the slits using a metal ruler, craft knife, and cutting mat.

4

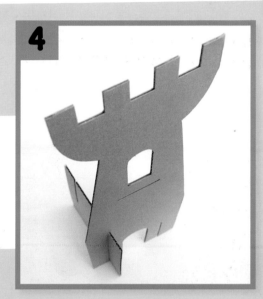

SLOT TOGETHER Once you have cut out all the shapes, slot them together to create the castle as shown in the photograph.

Crafty Tip

To keep your castle safe, you might even want to make an outer wall!

Once your castle is complete, let your little one decorate it. Stick to felt-tipped pens, marker pens, or crayons because paint will make the cardboard go soggy.

Kaleidoscope

KALEIDOSCOPES ARE TIMELESS TOYS AND YOU CAN MAKE A GREAT ONE FROM HOUSEHOLD PACKAGING. THIS PROJECT REQUIRES ADULT HELP, BUT CHILDREN WILL BE FASCINATED BY THE KALEIDOSCOPE'S CLEVER CONSTRUCTION AND THEN ASTOUNDED BY THE WONDERFUL COLORS AND SHAPES THEY SPY INSIDE.

WHAT YOU WILL NEED

- 1 clean, empty cookie or potato-chip tube with plastic lid
- Hammer and nail
- Double-sided mirror card (or aluminum foil glued onto card)
- Scissors
- Ruler
- Sticky tape
- Transparent plastic (from the recycling box)
- Pencil
- Tracing paper
- Small colorful transparent objects, such as beads

1

MAKE A HOLE Using a hammer and nail, pierce a hole in the metallic end of the tube. Make sure there are no rough edges.

2

MAKE A PRISM Create a reflective prism by cutting the mirror card into three strips. The strips should be ¾in (2cm) shorter than the length of your tube. To calculate the width of your strips, measure the diameter of your tube and times it by 0.866. Using sticky tape, stick the three strips of mirror card together to form a triangular prism.

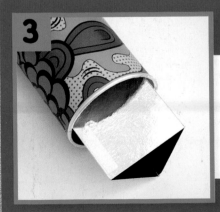

3

INSERT PRISM Push the prism into your tube so that it is flush at the metallic end. Secure in place using pieces of sticky tape.

4 TRACE CIRCLE Stand the tube on top of a piece of transparent plastic and, using a pencil, draw around the outside of the tube. Cut out the circle of transparent plastic and place it on top of the prism. Tape into place.

ADD BEADS Carefully pour your beads on top of the transparent plastic. Be careful not to overfill as the beads need to be able to move around.

FINISH LID Trace around the lid on tracing paper and cut out the circle. Use it to line the plastic lid for your tube to create a frosted effect. Put the lid back on the end of the tube. You can secure the lid using some tape or glue.

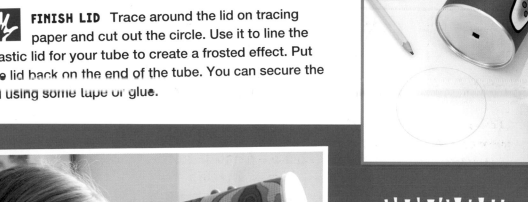

Crafty Tip

If you don't have an old cookie or potato chip tube, then a large cardboard roll will work just as well instead.

Lenny Lion Puppet

THIS CUTE KING OF THE JUNGLE IS LOTS OF FUN TO MAKE AND WILL KEEP YOUR CHILD HAPPILY OCCUPIED PAINTING, GLUING, TEARING, AND DRAWING. YOU CAN EASILY ADAPT THIS IDEA TO MAKE OTHER CREATURES—WHY NOT INVITE A FRIEND FOR A CRAFT AFTERNOON AND MAKE SOME COMPANIONS FOR LENNY?

WHAT YOU WILL NEED

- Templates on page 77
- Cardboard and cereal packaging
- Scissors
- Small cardboard tube
- Yellow acrylic paint
- Paintbrush
- Red and yellow tissue paper
- White/PVA glue
- Black pipe cleaners
- Craft pompom for nose
- Googly eyes
- Black marker pen

1

CUT OUT CIRCLES
Copy the templates on page 77 and cut out circles from cardboard, using cereal packaging for the larger circle.

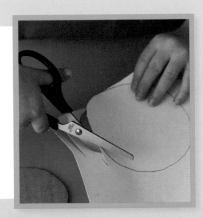

2

PAINT Using yellow paint, paint the cardboard tube and the larger circle, leaving the smaller circle for the face unpainted.

3

MAKE TISSUE PAPER STRIPS Cut or tear the red and yellow tissue paper into strips about 3 x ¾in (7 x 2cm) long.

GLUE TISSUE STRIPS Apply a generous amount of glue to the large painted circle and stick the strips of tissue paper in place all the way around, mixing up the colors as you go to make a magnificent mane.

4

5

ADD WHISKERS Now take the smaller, unpainted circle that you cut out in Step 1 and start to add the lion's features. Start with the whiskers: cut the pipe cleaners into six pieces about 2in (5cm) long and glue them to each side of the face.

6

ADD FACE Use a small dab of glue to attach the nose over the ends of the whiskers, and then stick on the googly eyes.

ADD MOUTH Use a black marker pen to draw on the lion's mouth—lions have mouths that look like an upside down "V."

7

8

ASSEMBLE To finish the lion, glue the face to the mane, then glue the top of the cardboard tube to the back of the head.

Shoebox Theater

THIS PROJECT TRANSFORMS A SHOEBOX INTO A STAGE! WITH A LITTLE BEHIND-THE-SCENES CUTTING, GLUING, AND PAINTING, YOUR CHILD CAN SOON CREATE A VENUE FOR FINGER PUPPET PERFORMANCES, OR SET THE STAGE FOR STORY-TELLING OR PLAYTIME WITH MINI FIGURES.

WHAT YOU WILL NEED

- Shoebox
- Craft knife and metal ruler
- Cutting mat
- Paint
- Paintbrush
- Felt-tipped pens or marker pens
- Small cardboard tube
- Scissors
- Sticky tape
- Sheets of colored paper
- Hole punch
- Pipe cleaner

1

CUT OUT STAGE Measure and mark a rectangle on the base of the shoebox, or cut freehand, with a border approximately 2in (5cm) wide at the top and 1¼in (3cm) wide on the sides and lower edge. Cut out the rectangle with a craft knife and cutting mat to leave a "window" for the stage. Keep the rectangle.

PAINT BOX Working on a covered surface, paint the whole box, front, back, top, and sides, including both sides of the rectangle of card cut away in Step 1. Let everything dry completely.

2

3

DECORATE Use felt-tipped or marker pens to draw patterns on the box to decorate it.

4

PAINT TUBE Use a different color to paint the outside of the cardboard tube. When it is dry, cut the tube into three pieces—these will make rings to help hold the stage curtains.

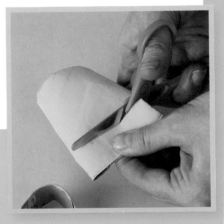

5

ATTACH RINGS Attach the rings to the rectangle of card along the underside of one long edge. Use sticky tape to keep them in place and position one at each end and one in the middle. Glue the rectangle to the top of the stage with the rings overhanging at the front.

6

MAKE CURTAINS Fold the sheet of colored paper into a concertina. Hold the folds together and punch a hole through all the folds. Repeat to make second curtain.

7

ATTACH CURTAINS Thread the pipe cleaner through the holes in one curtain, then through the first curtain ring. Fold the pipe cleaner down at the end to secure the curtain. Then thread it through the middle ring, the holes in the second curtain and the final ring, folding the end down to secure the curtain. The stage is now set!

Crafty Tip

You can attach stars, glitter, or sparkles to the borders of the stage if you want to add a bit of glamour to your production!

Spooky Rolls

WHAT YOU WILL NEED

- Small cardboard tubes
- Black and green construction paper
- Scissors
- Paper towel
- Double-sided sticky tape
- White/PVA glue
- Black marker pen
- Googly eyes

THESE FUN CHARACTERS ARE THE PERFECT HALLOWEEN PARTY CRAFT ACTIVITY. SIMPLY MADE FROM CARDBOARD TUBES AND A LITTLE PAINT, GLUE, AND PAPER, EACH CHILD CAN CREATE THEIR OWN MONSTER, EMBELLISHED WITH SPOOKY FACES.

1

PAINT TUBE Paint the outside of the cardboard tube with plenty of paint, making sure that you cover the entire surface. Let dry completely.

2

MAKE HAIR Cut a strip of black paper that is about 1½in (4cm) wide and long enough to go around the cardboard tube.

3

TRIM HAIR Use scissors to cut a jagged edge on one long side (so that it looks like the monster's hair). Alternatively, paint the hair around the top of the tube.

4

ATTACH HAIR Put a strip of double-sided tape along the top edge of the hair. Tape one end of the black paper strip to the top of the tube, wrap the paper around, and press to secure in place.

ADD EYES Add dabs of glue and attach googly eyes—the wonkier the better!

5

6

ADD MOUTH Use a black marker pen to draw a line with vertical "stitches" across it for the mouth.

MORE IDEAS For a Jack o'lantern, paint the tube orange and add green hair and cut-out triangles for the face. For a ghost, simply paint the tube white, add googly eyes, and draw on a mouth—whooooo!

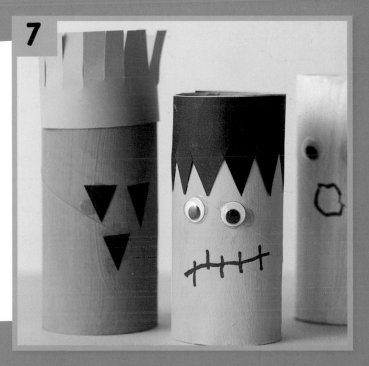

7

Homemade Chalk

A BLACKBOARD AND CHALK IS OFTEN A CHILD'S FIRST EXPERIENCE OF DRAWING—AND HALF THE FUN IS BEING ABLE TO RUB IT OUT AND START AGAIN! MAKING YOUR OWN SUPER-SIZED CHALK TOGETHER WILL ADD TO THE EXCITEMENT AND ENCOURAGE CREATIVITY.

WHAT YOU WILL NEED

- Cardboard tubes
- Masking tape
- Greaseproof baking parchment/waxed paper
- Scissors
- Paper towel
- Old plastic container
- 1 cup of water
- 1 cup of plaster of Paris
- Powdered tempera paint
- Stick or old wooden spoon for stirring

SEAL TUBES Tape up one end of each cardboard tube with masking tape, making sure that it is sealed all the way round.

LINE TUBES Cut pieces of greaseproof baking parchment/waxed paper and line the inside of each tube. Stand each tube, taped side down, on a level surface. Make sure you stand them on a piece of paper towel in case of any leaks.

MIX PLASTER OF PARIS Pour a cup of water into a plastic container, then sprinkle the plaster of Paris on top (generally it is a 1:1 ratio, but check the instructions on the package).

ADD POWDERED PAINT Add one heaped teaspoon of powdered paint to the mixture and give it a really good stir with a stick or old wooden spoon. If you want a deeper color, add more paint.

POUR INTO TUBE Help your child to pour the paint and plaster mixture into the prepared tubes and tap lightly to get rid of any air bubbles. Keep the tube upright and leave it in a quiet corner away from pets and little hands to set.

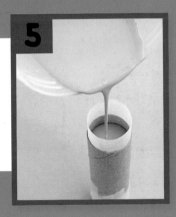

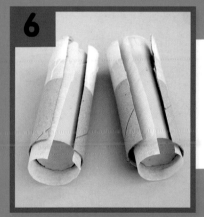

REMOVE TUBE When the plaster has set, you can remove the cardboard tube and lining paper. You will need to allow the chalk to dry fully for a few days before using.

Crafty Tip

If you feel your tube is too chunky, then cut it along the length, overlap the edges, and tape them back in place to reduce the diameter.

Greetings Card Box

TRANSFORM A FUN GREETINGS CARD INTO A FUN BOX! PERFECT FOR STORING BITS AND BOBS, OR AS A GIFT FOR GRANNY, THIS LITTLE BOX IS CONSTRUCTED FROM A FEW SIMPLE FOLDS AND BITS OF STICKY TAPE. A GREAT PROJECT TO MAKE TOGETHER, YOU'LL SOON HAVE A PRODUCTION LINE GOING!

WHAT YOU WILL NEED

- Square or rectangular greetings card with a big, bold image or pretty pattern
- Scissors
- Ruler
- Pencil
- Sticky tape

MARK GUIDELINES Cut the greetings card along the central fold so that you have two pieces the same size. Take the top of the card (the patterned piece), using a ruler and pencil, measure and mark the card with guidelines positioned ¾in (2cm) in from the edge on all four sides.

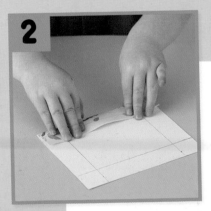

FOLD SIDES Following the pencil guidelines, fold the edge of the card in by ¾in (2cm) on all four sides of the card. Press along each fold to crease it in place.

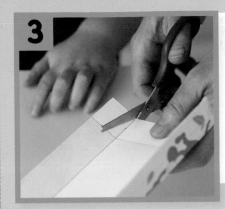

CUT EDGES With the card facing you, use scissors to cut along the short marked line in the bottom left corner, just to where it meets the corner of the marked square. Do the same in each corner of the card, cutting in from the outside along the ¾in (2cm) line to where it meets the corner of the square.

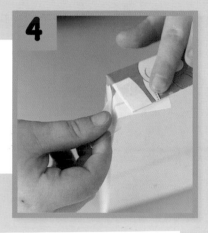

MAKE CORNERS Now fold and crease the square corners toward the inside. Refold the long outside edge, starting with the left edge. Use a piece of sticky tape to secure the edge to the folded corner square.

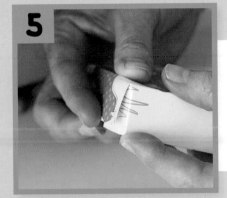

FINISH TOP Do the same thing in all three remaining corners, bringing up the edges of the card and securing the sides together with tape. The top of your greetings card box is finished.

MAKE BASE Take the back of the card (the part where you write a greeting). Repeat Steps 1 through 5 to make the base of the box. Place the top of the box over the base and you are finished!

Steam Locomotive

TRADITIONAL TOYS OFTEN STAND THE TEST OF TIME, AND THE OLD-FASHIONED STEAM LOCOMOTIVE IS ALWAYS POPULAR—THE SOUND EFFECTS ARE GOOD FUN, TOO! MAKE THIS ONE WITH A FEW ODDS AND ENDS FROM THE RECYCLING BOX AND A LICK OF PAINT, AND IT WILL BE STEAMING OFF ON IMAGINARY TRACKS IN NO TIME.

WHAT YOU WILL NEED

- Small cardboard pot
- Small carton or box
- Small cardboard tube
- Paint
- Paintbrush
- Scissors or craft knife
- White/PVA glue
- 6 foil cases, bottle tops, or shiny caps for wheels
- Craft sticks
- Cotton balls/cotton wool

PAINT CARDBOARD Paint all the cardboard pieces with a coat of paint, making sure that you cover the whole surface. You can use different colors for each part of the train, if you like. Let the paint dry and add another coat for a solid color to cover any packaging or print, if required.

ADD CHIMNEY When the paint is dry, use a craft knife to make a cross at one end of the box, about the same width as the cardboard tube. Slot in the painted cardboard tube to make the chimney.

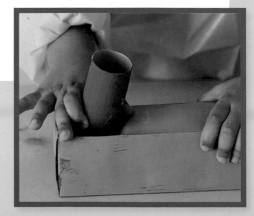

ADD WHEELS Use bottle tops, foil trays, or cut out cardboard circles for the wheels. Glue three wheels to each side of the box.

FINISH WHEELS To make the piston rod, glue on a craft stick across the center of the wheels on both sides.

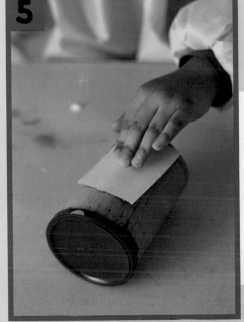

DECORATE ENGINE Cut out some rectangles of colored card or paper for the livery on the engine, and stick them to the side of the painted pot.

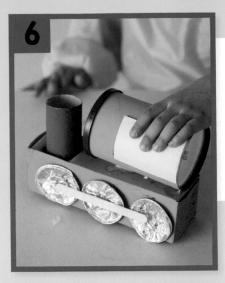

ADD ENGINE Now glue the decorated engine, or boiler, to the top of the box, on its side. Hold it in place until the glue has started to set.

ADD STEAM PUFFS Glue the cotton balls together and stuff inside the chimney to finish your engine with a puff of steam. Toot toot!

Crafty Tip

The train would be a great addition to the Toy Town project on page 68.

Flower Rolls

These pretty flowers are simple to assemble and can be used as party decorations or simply to adorn your child's bedroom. Use your favorite colors, making a pastel bunch for springtime or mix up the petals for a multicolored version.

WHAT YOU WILL NEED

- Small cardboard tubes
- Paint
- Paintbrush
- Scissors
- White/PVA glue
- Ribbon, twine, or string for hanging (optional)

1

PAINT TUBE Paint the cardboard tube all over, inside and out, in your chosen color. Let it dry completely.

CUT TUBE When dry, cut the painted tube into five equal parts, each one about 1in (2.5cm) wide. As you cut, the tube may get squashed from a circle shape to an oval shape—this is fine because you want an oval shape.

2

3

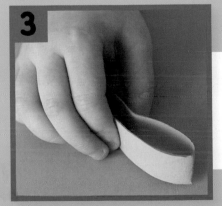

MAKE OVALS If the cut sections are not quite oval enough, squeeze them gently to flatten them slightly.

MAKE FLOWER SHAPE Now arrange your ovals into a flower shape on a flat surface. The ends of the ovals should be touching at the center.

GLUE TOGETHER Start with the bottom oval. Apply glue to the outside edges on the inner point. Stick this to the two ovals either side and then repeat with the two ovals at the top until they are all connected and you have a five-petal flower.

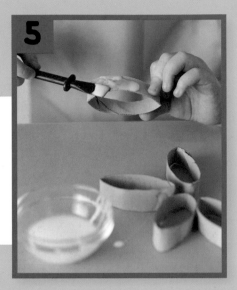

FINISH FLOWER Gently squeeze the glued edges together and hold for a few seconds. Allow to dry completely (this will take about 10 minutes).

THREAD HANGING LOOP If you would like to hang your flowers as decorations, thread a piece of narrow ribbon or twine through one of the petals and tie in a knot. Your flowers are ready to hang in your room, at a window, or transform a party room.

Cardboard Sandals

THIS PROJECT WILL APPEAL TO ALL THOSE WHO HAVE ALREADY DISCOVERED A LOVE OF SHOES! DESIGN AND MAKE YOUR OWN SWEET SANDALS FROM HOUSEHOLD PACKAGING—LOOK FOR BRIGHTLY COLORED CEREAL BOXES TO USE FOR THE STRAPS AND DECORATIONS, AND COLLECT CORRUGATED CARDBOARD FOR THE SOLES.

WHAT YOU WILL NEED

- Corrugated cardboard box
- Scissors
- Pen
- Decorated card packaging or greetings cards for straps
- White/PVA glue
- Gems or sequins (optional)

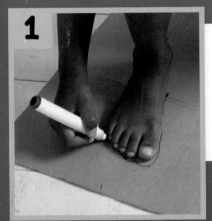

1 **TRACE FOOT** Ask your child to stand with their feet apart on a piece of the corrugated cardboard box. Draw around their feet, rounding off the toes.

2 **CUT OUT FEET TEMPLATES** Cut out the two feet shapes and mark them "L" and "R" for left and right. Use these as templates to draw around and cut out another pair of shapes from corrugated cardboard.

CUT STRAPS Cut two strips of card and lay them over the top of your child's feet to check that they will be long enough for the strap. Add 2in (5cm) to this measurement and cut to fit.

ADD STRAPS Bend each end of the strap under by 1 in (2.5cm) and glue it to the top of one of the soles. Glue the second sole onto the top of the first one—matching both left soles and right soles—and let dry.

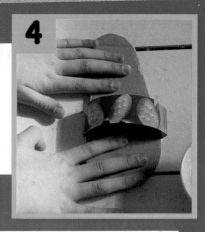

MAKE FLOWERS Cut out colorful shapes from packaging card or old greetings cards to make flower decorations. Cut one piece with curves to make the petals, and a smaller round piece for the center of the flower.

DECORATE Glue the shapes onto the straps—add some gems or sequins for extra sparkle if you like.

Crafty Tip

Make sure that the cardboard you use for the soles is not shiny so that they will not be slippery.

Toy Town

WHAT YOU WILL NEED

- Large carton or box (to create basic house)
- Acrylic paints
- Paintbrushes
- Scissors
- Scraps of paper for windows and doors
- White/PVA glue
- Cardboard for roof
- Sticky tape

THE RECYCLING BOX IS A GREAT SOURCE OF MATERIALS AND INSPIRATION. HERE, WITH LOTS OF PAINTING, CUTTING, AND GLUING, YOU CAN TRANSFORM EMPTY JUICE CARTONS, CEREAL BOXES, SHOEBOXES, AND CARDBOARD TUBES INTO BRIGHT BUILDINGS FOR A TOY TOWN. THIS IS A GREAT RAINY DAY ACTIVITY THAT YOU CAN ADD TO WHEN INSPIRATION STRIKES.

PAINT BOX Using a thick paintbrush, paint the box all over in your chosen color. Let the paint dry completely. For the best results, apply a second coat of paint and let it dry.

ADD DOOR AND WINDOWS Once the box is dry, cut out squares or rectangles of paper in contrasting bright colors to create doors and windows. For younger children, cut the squares for them to choose from; older children will enjoy cutting simple shapes. Use little squares of paper for the window panes. Glue them in place.

PAINT DETAILS Use a fine paintbrush and contrasting colored paint to add the window frames and door decorations. Allow the paint to dry completely.

4 🖐 **MAKE ROOF** Cut a piece of card measuring 9in (22cm) long by the width of the box. Fold the card three times to form a triangle shape and ask your child to help you to tape the edges together.

PAINT ROOF TILES Use a paintbrush to paint on the roof tiles. Allow the paint to dry completely before gluing the flat base of the roof to the top of the box to finish.

Collapsible Telescope

ALL NAUTICAL FANS AND TRAINEE PIRATES NEED A TELESCOPE IN THEIR DRESS-UP BOX. WITH FREE REIGN TO CUSTOMIZE IT IN THEIR FAVORITE COLORS AND FINISH IT WITH SPARKLY STICKERS, THERE'S LOTS TO HELP WITH AND THEY WILL SOON BE PUTTING THEIR FINISHED TELESCOPE TO GOOD USE, LOOKING FOR TREASURE ISLANDS OR GAZING AT THE STARS.

WHAT YOU WILL NEED

- 3 small cardboard tubes
- Scissors
- Sticky tape
- Paint
- Paintbrush
- Sheets of colored paper
- Ribbon
- Star stickers

PAINT TUBES Choose your favorite color and paint the outside of the cardboard tubes all over. Let them dry completely. You may need a second coat of paint to make sure all of the card is covered.

CUT TUBES Take two of the painted tubes and cut them down the length. Roll each tube to a slightly smaller circumference, so that one will fit inside the uncut tube, and the final tube fits inside the middle tube. Use sticky tape to join the sides when you are happy with the fit.

3

✋ **ADD RIBBON** Cut two lengths of ribbon about 7in (18cm) long. Tape one end of each ribbon on the bottom of the inside of the smallest tube, on opposite sides. Thread the ribbon through the tubes and tape it in place at the top, on opposite sides (see diagram on page 74). Trim the ends.

✋ **DECORATE** Cut strips of colored paper in three different colors and glue or tape them to the ends of each tube.

4

5

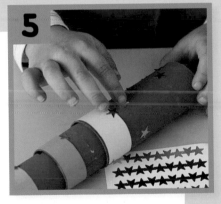

ADD STARS For a sparkly finishing touch, add star stickers all over the telescope.

Crafty Tip

For a pirate telescope, paint the tubes black and use glow-in-the-dark stickers.

Felt Story Board

THIS STORY BOARD WILL ENCOURAGE IMAGINATIVE PLAY, STORY-TELLING, PATTERN MAKING, AND CREATIVITY. IT'S VERY SIMPLE TO PUT TOGETHER AND YOU CAN USE EXISTING FELT SHAPES OR HELP YOUR CHILD TO MAKE THEIR OWN.

WHAT YOU WILL NEED

- Cardboard rectangle (re-use the spare piece from the Travel Desk on page 34)
- Scissors
- Sheets of felt in lots of colors
- Marker pen
- White/PVA glue

CUT OUT RECTANGLE Using scissors, cut out a cardboard rectangle. You can make it any size: try drawing around a piece of standard paper, or cutting out the side of a cereal box.

CUT FELT Put the cardboard on top of a piece of felt and draw around it. Cut out the felt about 1in (2.5cm) inside the marked line, to give you a border on the cardboard backing.

DECORATE Put a line of glue around the edge of the cardboard, about 1in (2.5cm) wide, and decorate the border with glitter. This will frame your pictures and make your stories look extra special! When the glitter is dry, glue the felt rectangle inside the decorated border on the cardboard.

4

EMBELLISH If you like, you can add even more sparkly decorations to the border, gluing them on top of the glitter.

MAKE FELT SHAPES Draw lots of different shapes on the felt. Draw around something round, such as a button or a cup, for circle shapes, and cut triangles, squares, and rectangles freehand. Younger children may need some help cutting shapes.

5

6

MAKE A STORY Arrange the shapes on your board in different patterns to make pictures or stories.

Crafty Tip

Put the Felt Story Board inside your Travel Desk (see page 34) for easy storage on road trips.

Templates

For help on using templates, see pages 12–13. All the templates are printed at actual size, apart from the Cardboard Castle and Apple Tree which are half size—enlarge them by 200 percent on a photocopier.

**Collapsible Telescope
Ribbon Diagram**
Page 70

**Apple Tree
(enlarge by 200 percent)**
Page 17

LEAF

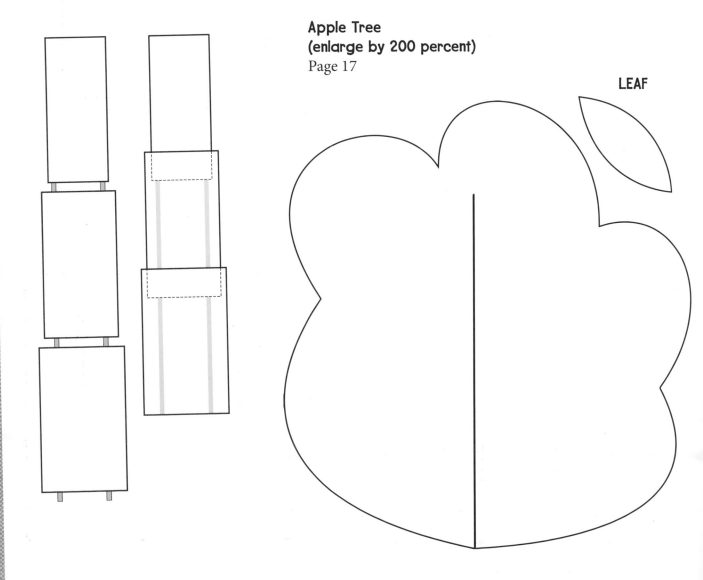

Cardboard Castle (enlarge by 200 percent)
Page 44

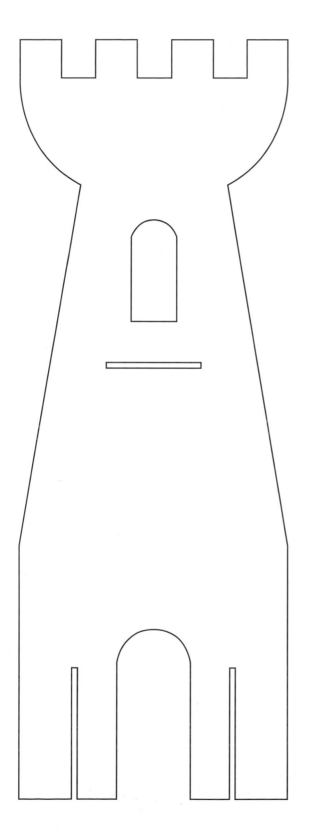

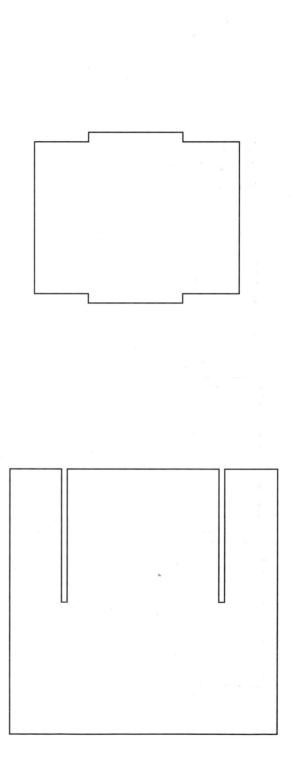

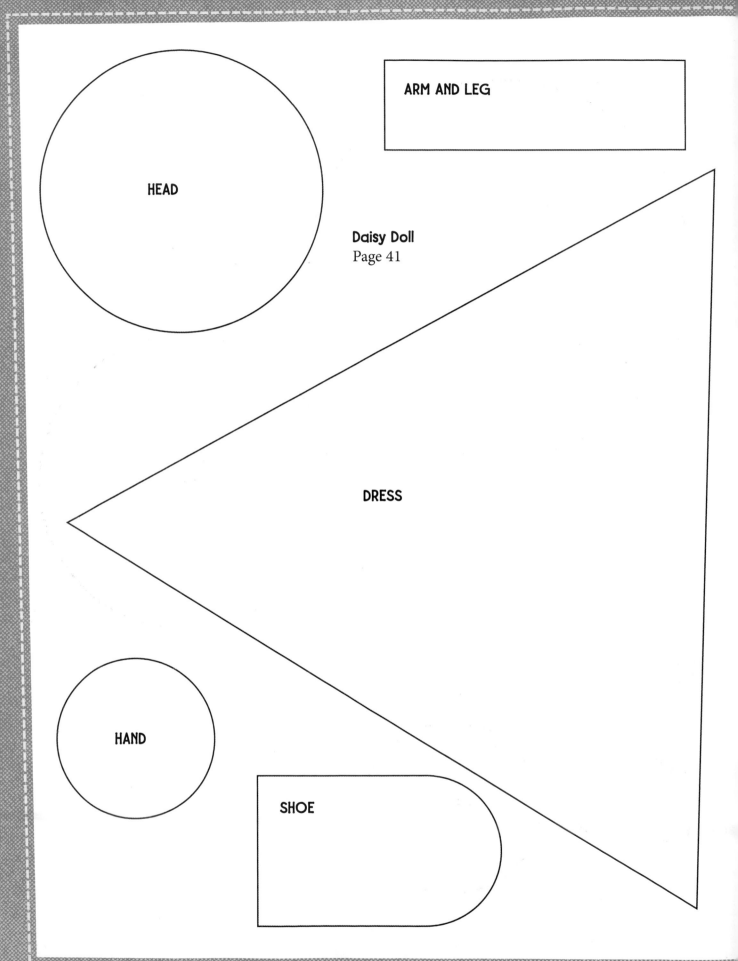

HEAD

ARM AND LEG

Daisy Doll
Page 41

DRESS

HAND

SHOE

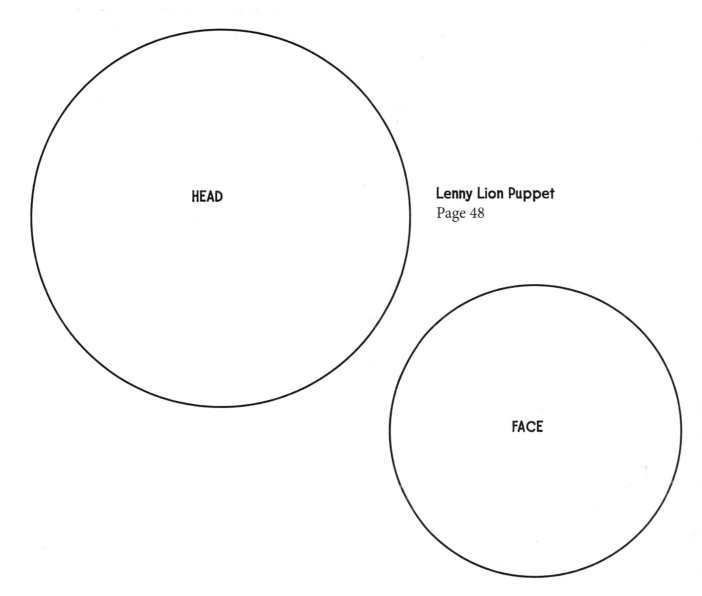

HEAD

Lenny Lion Puppet
Page 48

FACE

Egg Carton Creature
Page 14

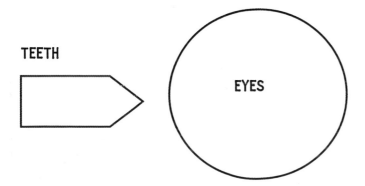

TEETH

EYES

Doll House Furniture
Page 30

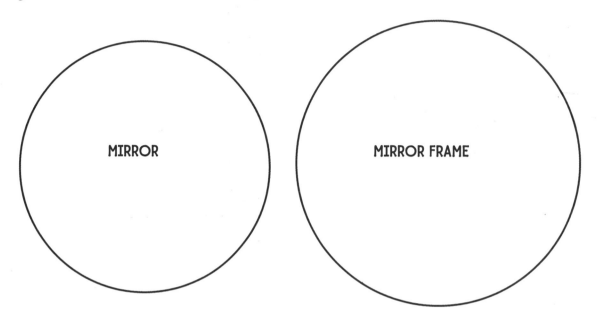

MIRROR

MIRROR FRAME

DRESSING TABLE TOP

Suppliers

US

A C Moore
www.acmoore.com

Create for Less
www.createforless.com

Darice
www.darice.com

Hobby Lobby
www.hobbylobby.com

Jo-ann Fabric & Crafts
www.joann.com

Michaels
www.michaels.com

Mister Art
www.misterart.com

Walmart
www.walmart.com

UK

Baker Ross
www.bakerross.co.uk

Early Learning Centre
www.elc.co.uk

Hobbycraft
www.hobbycraft.co.uk

Homecrafts Direct
www.homecrafts.co.uk

John Lewis
www.johnlewis.com

Mulberry Bush
www.mulberrybush.co.uk

Paperchase
www.paperchase.co.uk

The Works
www.theworks.co.uk

Yellow Moon
www.yellowmoon.org.uk

Index

CREDITS

PHOTOGRAPHY
Carolyn Barber pp. 44–47, 56–57
Terry Benson pp 1–43, 48–55, 58–65, 70–71,
Martin Norris pp. 72–73
Debbie Patterson pp. 66–67
Polly Wreford pp. 68–69

STYLISTS
Emily Breen pp. 1–43, 48–55, 58–65, 70–71
Emma Hardy pp. 66–67
Kate Lilley pp. 44–47, 56–57
Sophie Martell pp. 72–73
Catherine Woram pp. 68–69

PROJECT MAKERS
Emily Breen and Katie Hardwicke pp. 17–19, 26–28, 41–43, 48–53, 60–62, 70–71
Caroline Fernandez pp. 14–16, 22–23, 34–35, 36–37, 54–55, 58–59, 63–65, 72–73
Emma Hardy pp. 66–67
Kate Lilley pp. 24, 44–47
Catherine Woram pp. 20–21, 29–33, 38–40, 68–69

CICO Books would like to thank Megan Breen for the loan of her toys.